Andrew Staniland was born in Sheffield in 1959 and lives in London, where he works part time. His books so far have been self-published (poetry collections, narrative poems, prose-poem novels and plays).

titles by the author:

A Georgian Anthology
Letters Of Introduction (2018)
Playful Poems (2016)
Rhapsodies (2014)
The Perennial Poetry (2010)
Two Story Poems (2009)
Hymns, Films And Sonnetinas (2007)
New Poems (2006)
The Beauty Of Psyche (2005)
The Weight Of Light (2004)
Three Cine-Poems (1997)
Poems (1982-2004)
Four Plays (1994)

ANDREW STANILAND

A GEORGIAN ANTHOLOGY

published 2020 by
Andrew Staniland's Books

www.andrewstaniland.co.uk

© Andrew Staniland 2019

cover photos of Gelati monastery by the author

ISBN 9798642043875

Contents

I

In English poetry, the Caucasus 3

An eagle is far-seeing, ...4

There was an altar to Prometheus..4

What freed them first was fire, from the sun............................5

The smithies stole the secret from the sun, ...5

The other way of winning was with wine, ...5

I call upon the mother of the place, ...6

This bubble round a rock is blown by Barbale.........................6

To Dali, Dali, ...7

She shakes and shakes. The god of it..7

I call on Beri Bera, who is the..8

The rivers from the white peaks ran with gold, ...9

The king of Colchis asked 9

This river, the Rioni, is a rush, ...10

Medea was a maiden in 10

The gold we know today is from their graves, ...11

A seesaw for the Caesars and the Shahs, ...11

She came from Cappadocia..12

Saint Nino's cross of sticks, a wand of vine, ...13

The A script of the alphabet 13

Georgia, from George, the dragon-slaying saint, ...13

Georgia, from Georgics, agricultural, ...14

The secret name that only its own say..14

A horseman from his steppe, ...14

Great iron gates across a mountain pass 15

And in Gelati's gateway I..15

When little Georgia went from coast to coast, ...15

The greatest artist is unknown, ...16

A city hidden in a mountainside 16

I wander through the ruins of the palace....................................16

II

A poem that is long, like this, ...21

This is what love ideally is, ...21

The tiny, tiny, Tinatin,..22

A lion and a lioness, ...22

A knight sat sobbing by a stream, ...23

For Avtandil to fail to find 24

The sobbing knight was Tariel..24

Her name was Nestan-Darejan, ...25

The old king told the court his news, ...26

The third tall knight, a prince, was Pri-......................................27

Then Avtandil rode sadly home 27

He knew the madness of the moon. 28

With Nestan's knight too stressed now from 28

The woman was a merchant's wife......................................29

That night, her feelings were forlorn, ...30

And in the forest grotto's fort, ...31

The three knights, with three hundred men,..................32

They celebrated their success 32

III

The Georgian Lady, she was called, ...37

David the Sixth was king of Georgia when 38

In Samarkand, the tomb of Tamerlane, ...38

The drum of armies and the eerie creak..........................40

A steep slate crag looks like a castle and.......................40

When Russian writers saw the Caucasus, ...40

The log fire in his study blazes, ...41

General. Poet. And why not?...41

What might the Mtkvari river write, ...42

A shepherdess was storm-struck on 42

Ah, attar in the air, a crims-..43

I wish I was the rain, the rain, ... 44

In that hard highland, where the win- 44

A sprig of violets sprang up 45

A man who eats the meat of snakes, ... 46

Those mountain men, the Khevsurs, wore 47

The few days that I stayed there for, so beautiful a base, ... 47

The house had seven wooden chests, ... 48

A cowbell concert through the guesthouse win- 49

Shall we talk too about the turs, ... 49

IV

Some sort of summer colony, I thought, ... 53

Something was wrong. The driver drew the reins. 54

Wilder than Wilde was, Titsian, a pasha of a po- 54

Nothing, if not for love, is, not 55

And on the holy mountain they are howling at the moon, ... 55

He said that poets don't write poems, they 56

Georgians beware of Georgians. They were their 56

His pen's nib was a songbird's beak, ... 57

The night and I can now confide. That mountain has a 57

Galaktioni, what a poet, was 58

Shutting out Russian power, circuits shorting, ... 60

A prophet for a president? 60

They shouted it across the street, ...60

The roses were romantic. The reforms 61

And then there was a war, a little war, ...61

A grande salle (ah, but flakey paint), a long brass chandelier, ..62

I see an open-ended house, ...62

And in the maddest minibus, ...63

I stride out/slow down on the famous four 63

Notes 67

Reading 75

A Georgian Anthology

I

⏋

In English poetry, the Caucasus
    Calls up (and seldom is called up) a place,
The point (or points) of which, as I assess
    It, as an image, is quite simple. Ic-
Y and remote and desolate. A source
    Of similes for poets to police,
        Of eagles and, alone upon the peaks,
        Prometheus. The silence of it speaks.

The Alps are the ineffable and on
    The Grand Romantic Tour, that is, that all
The awe on offer, easy awe, is one
    That is seen safely, thank you, from the tal-
Ismanic mass of Jura or Mont Blanc
    To mint sheets in a chalet or hotel.
        Of course the Caucasus is more remote
        Than this. Its absence is what we emote.

I stand amidst the flowers in a high
    Meadow, with mountains round me, to the south
Blue haze, the north black rock, a bank of hay
    That two men scythe in time (the old man scyth-
Ing three in four), a hut, with halter, hoe,
    Cows cooling, that a pond's mud seems to soothe.
        This is in summer, certainly, but still,
        The wilderness is worked here by the will.

Thousands of towers, full of families,
    Were in the highlands in their heyday. They
Were wealthy, hiring artists, those of these
    Gilt icons and great carvings, well-armed, though
The crags were fortresses with icy ease,
    Almost a Swiss-style fastness, stone vaults the
        Jewels of Georgia went in when campaigns
        Were desolating its warm lowland plains.

                            略

    An eagle is far-seeing,
Riding the heat trails, then, ah, breakfast in the beak.

    An eagle is foreseeing,
Reading the entrails of that prophet on the peak.

                            略

There was an altar to Prometheus
    In Athens, where a race of torches ran
From, in a thorny thicket, for the use
    Of the Academy. *With thanks, from man.*

That was the only one. Elsewhere in Greece,
    The gods who had an altar in their name
Were all Olympian. The most transgress-
    Ive even had them. They had won the game.

I wonder if, below Mount Kazbek, where
    The church is now, so beautiful and bleak,
There was a temple to the titan there,
    That virtuous volcano on the peak?

&

What freed them first was fire, from the sun
    And the soft valleys to where ores were un-
        Der snow and rock. The conquests had begun.

&

The smithies stole the secret from the sun,
    A sword arising from its fiery run
        And finally a flintlock for a gun.

&

The other way of winning was with wine,
    The culture of it crawling like a vine
        Across a wall. Entangle and entwine.

&

I call upon the mother of the place,
    adgilis deda, of this mountain, of
That valley, in it as a spectral plus,
    That we can never see or know enough.

The mother of the place appears for us,
    As if a shift of silver or of pearls
Shimmies the light, a brightness and a buzz,
    In answer to our obstinate appeals.

The mother will protect us from the place,
    An icy cliff edge or a gnarly maze,
And if it worsens, if we worship less,
    The mother will protect the place from us.

This bubble round a rock is blown by Barbale.
That bauble in the blue is hers, is Barbale's.

That ball with burning barbs is hers, is Barbale's.
This babbling of bells is all for Barbale.

A burble in the belly is by Barbale.
A bellow by a bull below her is for Barbale.

A bale is by her. Stubble charring is by Barbale.
A bowl of ears of barley is for Barbale.

To Dali, Dali,
Duly, daily,
   Amidst the herds,
   A hymn is heard,
      That horns are holy, hooves are holy,
         And all that she has willed
      Holy, the holy wild.

Daintily, Dali
Will dally, dally
   Amidst the rocks,
   Her yellow locks
      Drying, a hunter in the hilly
         Highlands, who will discover
      Her, dying, her dying lover.

❧

She shakes and shakes. The god of it
   Is in her, almost bursting out.
Then after this prophetic fit
   Is groggy, like a birthing goat.

She speaks. The syllables of sound
   Are sibylline, a secret tongue
That when translated will astound
   Us with tomorrow's sacred song.

❧

I call on Beri Bera, who is the
  Berry bearer, the bushel bringer, for
  Abundance until spring from autumn's store.

In all the mountains, I call Mamberi,
  The master of the wolves, for teeth to smile
  Like icicles, along a weary mile.

In all the cowsheds, I call Michpa, he
  Who husbands, more from not so much, as now,
  For warmth in winter, milk amidst the snow.

I call on mindful Mindort Batoni,
  In all the valleys, for the right to tread
  A trail through flowers, yellow, blue and red.

I call on Ochopintre, who is the
  Goddess's goatherd, for the only way
  Out of a forest, hoof prints in the hay.

I call on all the gods of earth, as they
  Are quickening a root, a rock, a riv-
  Er, for their tongues to lick us so we live.

ട

ნ

The rivers from the white peaks ran with gold,
    Like sunlight in the water, how the spokes
        Spin in it. Wealth was breaking from the east.

A skin was stretched across a stream, an old
    Shepherd's skilfulness, sifting it for specks,
        Then set to dry and shaken. Gold got fleeced.

                        ès

The king of Colchis asked
    If Jason had the balls
    To bully his two brazen, blazing bulls,
        Beneath a yoke, to bid them yield?
            Medea made a bull-proof medicine.

What Jason then was tasked
    With was to sow the field
    The bulls had ploughed with teeth, a dragon's teeth,
    That killer robots, sword and sheath,
        Sprang from. Medea's stone made them insane.

A bigger dragon basked
    Against a rocky crease,
        Tail twitching, belly bloated, like a shield
    Glistening, gilded by the fleece.
        Medea made it nod off in the sun.

This river, the Rioni, is a rush,
    Even in August, from the Caucasus
        To Kutaisi. And a clayey grey.

It was the Phasis, famous for the flush
    Of pheasants from its sides. As raucous as
        A brace of Bronze Age princes after prey.

ཞ

Medea was a maiden in
    The meadows, culling coloured heads,
Like medals, for their medicine,
    The dews of yellows, blues and reds.

Medea was a medium,
    Who moodily made into words
The mumble of a temple drum,
    The sunset-stencilled wings of birds.

Medea was a midwife, as
    The queens of Colchis always were,
In an unsullied house of ease,
    Cutting the soft, still-pulsing wire.

Medea wasn't mad. She killed
    The faithless Jason's little heirs
So calmly that the sun god called
    Her from midheaven. He was hers.

ཞ

The gold we know today is from their graves,
   Such as the goblets on which tales are told
      Of the shamanic, animals and shrines.

More metals and the good wood of the groves
   Were why they were so wealthy, which they toiled
      For, smelting ore in early iron mines.

ಎ

A seesaw for the Caesars and the Shahs,
   These little kingdoms in between
      Them, that they asked (or forced)
To feed their legions / their immor-
              tal horsemen or to lick their shoes,

As playgrounds for the empires, from the Great
   Caucasus to the Small, between
      Seas B and C, were forced
To fight for them or bow before
              their gods. Like boys an ogre ate.

ಎ

She came from Cappadocia
 As common Nino, calling them
  To her good God. And when a waif
Got achier and achier,
 She healed him with her hair shirt's hem,
  As those who watched it would vouchsafe.

The queen was also ill, an angst
 The court physicians couldn't treat,
  Chilling her *chakras*, hard and coarse,
That Nino held her cross against.
 The angry king, though, howled a threat
  Of death to Nino and divorce.

A killing party by the king,
 Beating a wild pig through a wood-
  Land, was eclipsed, a loss of light
In the king's eyes, who, panicking,
 Told Nino's God the things he would
  Do now, if it was not too late.

He ordered buildings to be built,
 In which the new professionals
  Administered the rites by rote.
So Nino went on. Sobs were spilt
 Beneath a bush, with thorns like nails,
  Until the spirit cleared her throat.

Saint Nino's cross of sticks, a wand of vine,
Isn't a straight cross. Straightness is in vain.

It is her hair that lashes it, her hair,
A few long strands of it. And it is here.

༄

The A script of the alphabet
    Was capital, to cut in stone.
The B script, a bit simpler but
    Still scriptural, was to atone.

The cursive C was cavalier,
    A line that charged across the page,
And with it came, as quick and clear,
    A layman's literary age.

༄

Georgia, from George, the dragon-slaying saint,
    Although the dragon, by its notness, sent
        Him out of isness too. To represent.

༄

Georgia, from *Georgics*, agricultural,
   Because its baskets, in the sun, were all
      Blushing so sweetly. Eat this. It is real.

❧

The secret name that only its own say
   Is *sakartvelo*, from *kartveli*. They
      Call it their country. So may it still stay.

❧

   A horseman from his steppe,
      A spearman from his heat,
They burnt Tbilisi and they built Tbilisi.

   A herder from his steep
      And icily enamelled height,
They burnt Tbilisi and they built Tbilisi.

   A scruple didn't stop
      A hunter from his hut,
They burnt Tbilisi and they built Tbilisi.

❧

Great iron gates across a mountain pass
    That has a thousand guards, a pass of peace,
        Though who, the Persian or Byzantine, pays?

❧

And in Gelati's gateway I
    See David's gravestone in the ground,
His epitaph worn down. May I
    Say this? The great are never grand.

He wanted to be walked upon,
    To go to church, to go to school,
And those who did so have since gone,
    To be each step by which we scale.

❧

When little Georgia went from coast to coast,
    It built the best, the monasteries, cast-
        Les, that it ever would. There was a cost.

❧

The greatest artist is unknown,
    Of murals (that are scorched and scratched)
Of hermits, heroes of a throne,
    That no Romantic name has matched.

The sculptor also is unknown,
    Of an old brute, a budding bough,
On columns and a coping stone,
    That God there could not but allow.

        ê

A city hidden in a mountainside
    Was safe from all the soldiers and a sudd-
        En spring of steel that spilled down, spears and
                swords.

        ê

I wander through the ruins of the palace
    Where Queen Tamar once reigned and see her figure,
A Georgian Gloriana or a Pallas
    Athene in her armour. Breathing bigger,
She brandishes her rod, a female phallus,
    That smashed in battle, twice, the Seljuk ogre.
        These ruins are romantic, a sad scene,
        Frogs in a cistern, me, the misty queen.

Her consort was a drunken Russian prince,
    So she decoupled, smacking down his coup,
And after that, arranged by those old prunes,
    Her council, chose her own with whom to coo,
An Alan prince, who loved the slap of reins
    Until the end, commanding at her cue.
        Now her remains are nowhere to be seen,
        As if she is the once-and-future queen.

That Rustaveli was inspired by her
    To write his knightly epic is the same
As Spenser and his fellow poets were
    By their Queen Muse, a courtly art the aim
Of which, if not for personal prefer-
    Ment, was a fantasising of her fame,
        A setting for it, somewhere rude and green,
        Since when the greatest ruler is a queen.

                      ea.

II

ट

A poem that is long, like this,
        is what a poet ought to write,
As brilliant as it is long,
        because the source of it is bright.
The song of it is confident
        and its conceit is not contrite,
I.e. (and true of any song)
        by being beautiful, be right.

※

This is what love ideally is,
        the light that is above a fire,
Shimmering, almost immater-
        ial, that even from afar,
Impresses on the eye that, like
        a wise and good judge, it is fair,
As if it is what fire is from
        and also what a fire is for.

※

The tiny, tiny, Tinatin,
   An old king's only child,
Was a Tamar, the timing in attain-
      Ing sovereignty over all,
   The warmth with which she smiled,
      Like sunlight on a southern wall.

If Avtandil, a handsome knight,
   Had told her of his love,
He would have used the terms that are innate
      In any knight, her arrows through
   His armour, oh, his cruel ov-
      Erthrower… He said nothing, though.

ঌ

A lion and a lioness,
         as cute, as cubs, as one another, are
As fearlessly imperious,
         for their parental pride to rear.
A lion has a manly mane,
         a lower, let-it-all-out roar,
A lioness, though, as a ru-
         ler, is as ruthless, if more rare.

ঌ

A knight sat sobbing by a stream,
    His eyes rimmed red with fiery tears,
As if at any one extreme
    Another element appears.

He wore a speckled cap and cape.
    It was a panther's pelt. A male.
His armour scraping, gasps escap-
    Ing, tears bumped pearls stitched on the mail.

What ailed the pale knight loitering?
    The king was curious, concerned.
His own knights called him, clattering.
    He mounted his tall horse and turned

Away. A look of loneliness.
    It wasn't courteous. The knights
Confronted him. A neck, a nose
    Of theirs was broken, all those knights

Against him, like a phantom of
    A panther's fury, that destroyed
Them all. Then, through the murk, the mauve,
    He galloped headlong into a void.

And Tinatin told Avtandil
    The way that he would win her love.
Find him. An order. An ordeal.
    If he was humanly alive.

For Avtandil to fail to find
        him seemed, if not his fault, his fate,
Until he saw him from afar,
        as three knights fleeing from defeat
To him had told him, so he foll-
        owed to a forest grotto's fort…
What was the way to greet him, not
        to face his fury and to fight?

        ❧

The sobbing knight was Tariel
    And Avtandil was sobbing too…
These two, who with a stare, a yell,
      Sent foes, an army, to the ends
    Of Asia, to the seas, these two
        In one another's arms as friends.

Who was the subject of his sobs?
    The lady Asmat led the tall
Knights, subtly, shrewdly, through the obs-
      Tacles of their own stubbornness,
    For Tariel to tell his tale
        Of stabbing love, a high-born lioness.

        ❧

Her name was Nestan-Darejan,
    another kingdom's only heir
And who, a genie of a gust
    under an awning, gasping, *ah*,
To Tariel, in those green grounds,
    was as astounding as an aur-
A of the sun through arcs of rain,
    as iridescent in the air.

And Nestan wrote to Tariel,
    in ink that was an August sky's,
That he would be her husband, that
    he was already in her eyes,
But she was not impressed at all
    by adolescent sobs and sighs,
She wanted him to win a war
    for her, then he would be her prize.

So Tariel marched eastward with
    an iron horde of horse and foot,
Into an ambush by a khan,
    inflicting an absurd defeat
On him, and marched home with a line
    of those still living who had fought
Him, laden with the khanate's wealth.
    They feted his heroic feat.

The old king told the court his news,
    Nestan would wed a shah's son now,
A union that he would use
    To be a victor by a vow.

She shrieked at teary Tariel,
    She was betrayed, she was betrothed,
Like lightning through a tree's aerial,
    Kill him, this little boy she loathed.

So Tariel tore through his tent,
    Slamming the sleepy shahling's skull
Against a stick and, as he went,
    Salting the watchmen with a scowl.

He sent a message to the court
    From his cliff fortress, a rejoin-
Der to the king, but Asmat brought
    Him news that Nestan-Darejan,

Whom her demonic aunt had tied
    Up and tormented, was a burd-
En on a boat, that a night tide
    Would eat, some offal overboard.

ф

The third tall knight, a prince, was Pri-
　　　don, smiling with such pride to share
The wealth of his small city with
　　　a friend, with Tariel, a sheer
Ardour-in-armour for him, who
　　　had healed him from an archer's shower…
He said that, on a headland's height,
　　　he had seen Nestan shipped ashore.

Then Avtandil rode sadly home
　　And told the tale of Tariel
To Tinatin, to whom
　　　He had been true and now, he told her as he frowned,
　　　　He had to be as true
　　　As a knight had to be to his new friend.

And swiftly, silently he rode
　　Away, without a royal
Warrant to do so, on a worn-out road
　　　Towards him, oh, that one who was so dear,
　　　　A tall, straight aloe tree.
　　　He was an errant knight. And he would err.

He knew the madness of the moon.
        He knew the mildness of the moon.
He knew its cycles, what that month-
        ly madness was that made him moan
And on a still, unclouded night
        this mildness in his mind might mean…
He knew the night's white queen was one
        with Tinatin, one mind, one moon.

ଏ

With Nestan's knight too stressed now from
    The loss of her to look for her,
It was his friend who set off, roam-
    Ing, like a hunter for a hare.

He sought out Pridon by the sea,
    Who showed him to the very grain
Of sand the shoreline where he saw
    Her. Where they shipped her from again.

And he was shipped by merchants to
    A port where sailors drank and diced,
Where tall ships moored for tugs to tow
    And where he, madly, was seduced.

ଏ

The woman was a merchant's wife
          whose husband was away on trade,
So when a knight, much younger than
          her, loped in with a long, strong stride,
She had to host him on her own
          and be unstinting, as she tried
To be, the sun's heat on her o-
          live skin, on which a finger strayed.

The hostess, Patman, was a match
          for Avtandil, to whom she wrote
That he was like a sun, a rose,
          and how her heart was overwrought…
He told himself, oh, it was for
          a reason, it was reasonably right,
She was a woman who might har-
          bour some ship's bearings for his route.

And when he whispered in her hair
          the wherefore of his wandering,
She stared out at the stars and told
          him who they were and how they wrang-
Led Nestan-Darejan and though
          she knew what she was squandering,
She was unstinting in this too.
          She told him and she wasn't wrong.

That night, her feelings were forlorn,
    As Patman with a sigh
Through a high casement, perilously lean-
    Ing, saw the moon shine on the sea.

The moon was Nestan-Darejan,
    A silver wake from her small boat
Beaching below, as if regen-
    Erated by the sea's soft beat.

The merchant's wife sent slaves to buy
    Her, but the sailors wouldn't sell,
So they paid them with knives… The bay
    Was black, the pearl prised from its shell.

And Patman hid her in her house,
    On pillows no day ever dried,
Her eyes, in this immodest, dous-
    Ing them, the moon's despotic tide.

The merchant, though, his tongue well-wined,
    Touted her to the king, a won-
Der of a wife, to be assigned
    To his good-looking, warlike son.

Nestan was not his wagging dog.
    She paid the palace eunuchs pearls
For rags and crept between its grogg-
    Y guests, beyond its pillared piles,

Then galloped on a tall black horse
    Patman had harnessed for her flight
Across a steppe of grass and gorse
    On which a moonlight seemed to float,

Where brigands grabbed her, as a trib-
    Ute to the Kaji queen, whereby
There would be new stock for the tribe,
    A little nephew's bride-to-be.

The Kajis' castle was as mass-
    Ive as a mountain, glacier-girded.
The way in was a thin crevasse
    That thousands of their swordsmen guarded.

The queen, though, was away for now,
    With all of her worst sorcerers,
So now it was, and almost how,
    For knights who wanted war with hers.

ঌ

And in the forest grotto's fort,
        where Tariel had fought off fiends,
He found a fortune's finely frett-
        ed metals and amongst these finds
Was armour of a fiendish force
        for fighting Kajis, forty fronds
In filigree, with fiery swords
        from fiendish forges for his friends.

ঌ

The three knights, with three hundred men,
    Rode hard by night through Kaji lands,
The castle's cliffs ahead, that moon-
    Light metalled. A stark stump still stands.

At dawn they cantered closer, peace-
    Ful pilgrims in the sentries' eyes,
Then spurred and speared, with piercing pace
    And with the power of surprise.

Within the gates they wheeled in three
    Squadrons, slashing and slashing, slay-
Ing them, three hundred heroes thre-
    Shing thousands, like thick straw they lay.

The castle keep was quiet now
    And on its steps, amidst all this,
What Tariel had killed to know,
    Nestan knew too, her kiss, his kiss.

❧

They celebrated their success
      for seven days and seven nights,
A wine of singing in their throats
      that spilt extraordinary notes,
Then Tinatin and Nestan-Dar-
      ejan were married to their knights,
With many gifts, worth nothing on
      a scale with their silk nuptial knots.

Asmat was asked to choose a hus-
      band too, a consort for a queen,
Pridon, perhaps, but she refused
      and ruled as an ascetic.
                                When
The friends, in turn, were hosts then, there
      was non-stop feasting, with huge quan-
Tities of pomegranates, roast-
      ed game and aromatic wine.

They answered armies that advanced
      on any one of them as one,
With such unerring aim an er-
      a that was prosperous was won,
At peace, between the sun's three thrones,
      between the peacock and the swan,
Between the eagle and the bear,
      for their successors, on and on.

III

G

The Georgian Lady, she was called,
    Granddaughter of the great Tamar
    And also, after her, Tamar,
Who, when a sultan wooed her, wasn't walled
    In his harem, a true Tamar.

The Georgian Lady was the sun
    That shone on Seljuk coins above
    A lion, yes, she shone above
The sultan's lion, as the tropic sun
    Did, as a tender of his love.

The Georgian Lady loved the poor
    And liked the plump ambassadors.
    She liked, with the ambassadors,
To peg their principles and, with the poor,
    The price of bread at bakers' doors.

The Georgian Lady was a friend
    To Rumi, a true follower,
And at his final poem's end
Funded a mausoleum for her friend.
    Nobody funded one for her.

David the Sixth was king of Georgia when
    David the Seventh was as well. They ruled
Two Georgias, West and East, and neither won
    The Mongol wars in which they got embroiled.

David the Sixth's son, Constantine the First,
    Was monstered by a brother and by low-
Ly lords. This brother's son, his little fist,
    Was subject to King George the Fifth below.

David the Seventh was succeeded by
    Five or six kings appointed by a khan
Or two, until King George the Sixth, a boy,
    Whom George the Fifth succeeded. Quickly, cann-
      Ily, he kicked the khanate out, then quelled
        The lords. One kingdom. Whose new laws were
                        quilled.

※

In Samarkand, the tomb of Tamerlane,
    That beautiful blue bulb, those sculpted scales,
Was the still centre of a ruthless reign,
    Round which was a circumference of skulls
From other cities' sackings. They were slain
    If they weren't artisans. He used their skills
      On the new monuments of Samarkand,
        Mosques and madrasas, gilded, glazed and grand.

He summoned Hafiz to debate a verse
    About the worth, in cities, of a mole
On someone's skin, somewhere, and what was worse,
    They were *his* cities. Hafiz said, the hole,
For nothing too, that this put in his purse
    Was why he was so poor, a poem's toll,
        And Tamerlane hand-tipped him for his wit,
        A silkworm's purse with gold coins filling it.

Georgia was on the border, in the way,
    Between his orders and the Golden Horde,
So eight times he invaded it, like hay
    His horses trampled, eight times, with his sword,
It was depopulated, devasta-
    Ted. Ruins, that would never be restored,
        On maps look like red edits on a story,
        Was town, was village, was a monastery.

There was a warning, too, to the unwise.
    The airing of his corpse would cause a curse,
Which Operation Barbarossa was
    And which was halted in the Caucasus
Before it got to Baku's wells, the woes
    Of both men's Tamerlanesque massacres
        Worsening even after, with a word,
        His long, lame skeleton was reinterred.

The drum of armies and the eerie creak
    Of an old earthquake echo in a crook-
        Ed castle, in a runoff through a crack.

A steep slate crag looks like a castle and
    A castle's stump looks like a crag. The land
        Grows castles. As its outcrops they all end.

When Russian writers saw the Caucasus,
    They were the same as we were with the Alps,
In Georgia too, as much in awe as us
    In Italy, the classical collapse
        Of the old walls, the warmth of it, the wine,

Exotic as it was, with tasselled things,
    So not so Swiss or Roman, an expanse
For Orientalist imaginings,
    As Pushkin's were, of rebels and romance,
        Or Lermontov's, his high and jagged line.

The log fire in his study blazes,
    As if it is a winter's night.
The leather armchair where he lazes
    Is so damned hot it might ignite.

Thus jesting, sheet by sheet, he feeds
    A dozen years of his best verse,
That, line by line, as if it reads
    Them first, the laughing fire devours.

❧

General. Poet. And why not?
    Patriot. Tsarist office… Er.
        He was romantic (so am I)
And an administrator. What
    Else? He was quite a connoisseur
        Of wine and singing. With an army eye.

So he could write *A Toast*, about
    A long night on a battlefield,
        About non-literary things,
Like tactics, an outrageous rout,
    What had succeeded, what had failed
        Them, in the lineage of Georgian kings.

❧

What might the Mtkvari river write,
   In one long line along the valley of its verse?
It writes about the highlands it reveres,
    The rocks through which it rings like bells,
      The tributary gorges
      With tributes that are Georgia's,
   The floodplain's fields and orchards it loves as
                              much as fells.

What might the Mtkvari river write,
   In one long line along the valley of its verse?
It writes about the writers it reveres,
    Like Baratashvili, who wrote
      Upon its banks about
      The springs of angst and doubt,
    When inspiration was a river in his throat.

                         ❧

A shepherdess was storm-struck on
   Mount Kazbek with her father's flock.
The sky was black, the lightning shone,
   The thunder was a seismic shock.

She sheltered with a holy her-
   Mit in his cell, that hummed a hymn,
And told him, seeing how his hair
   Was knotted, what was what with him.

She told him that the world was where
   More glory was, so many loves,
And on that mountain he should wear
   Much warmer clothes, a hat and gloves.

The shepherdess then fell asleep
   Beside the embers in the grate,
Becoming, in her dreams of sheep,
   A sunset-silhouetted gate.

And in the morning she awoke
   Alone and ran to find her flock.
The hermit, like a stag night joke,
   Lay naked, bleeding, on a rock.

              ❧

Ah, attar in the air, a crims-
   On rose is opening its lips
And closing as the old day dims,
   Into an odourless eclipse.

I hear the *chi-chi* that a night-
   Ingale is singing in a wood.
It is a disembodied note,
   Thanks to the night, the thick black wood.

I see a star that shines so far
   Above me (shrunken, if not slov-
Enly, unfit for such fine fare)
   That it must be the one I love.

              ❧

I wish I was the rain, the rain,
    A shower from the sky,
Oh, I would open up and overrun
    A flower that is coy.

I would be raindrops, in whose eyes
    A little world is seen,
A world of joy and genuine surprise,
    That splashes, oh, so soon.

I would be snowflakes in the win-
    Ter, feathering the air.
A flake is faith-like, oh, its own exquisite one
    And then it isn't there.

And I would not be one who dri-
    Ly cowers and complains
At what is outside, oh, not be so wry,
    Because it rains, it rains.

                ès

In that hard highland, where the win-
Ter months were many, blue-grey floes
Bottling up the river's head,
Where winds hissed through the passes, winn-
Owing the gristle off the dead
Of their long-time, now-Muslim foes,
Shot as they rode off from a raid,
Where landslides holed the hillside road,
And where the animals that kill,
The eagles and the wolves, and those

That eat the carrion, the crows
And vultures, taught them all their skill,
The Christianity they preached
Was only the Old Testament,
Implacable, implacable,
With knives, for which the priest still reached
To celebrate the sacrament
With sacrifices, a black bull-
Calf or a ewe, a slab and trough
By the church wall, that horns hung off,
And if a man should follow Christ
Through any charity he felt
Towards a Chechen or a Kist,
No one forgave him for his fault,
His house was knocked down, his few herds
Were seized, his sacks of seeds for sow-
Ing, and they sent him, with his wife
And children, like a clutch of birds,
Across a high pass in the snow,
Under the eyes of vultures, woef-
Ul wolves, beside the blue-grey floes,
Unto the judgement of his foes.

ஆ.

A sprig of violets sprang up
   Near an old beech trunk's northern side
Where two roots branched and in that gap,
   Never seeing the sun, they died.

ஆ.

A man who eats the meat of snakes,
Cooked in a cauldron with a herb,
Will be new-skinned, a surge that makes
New senses, as a happy harb-
Inger, who hears the songs of birds,
The languages of animals,
And understands the warbled words,
The wisdoms of their yelps and mewls,
And he will sip the dew and pass
Through mountain meadows in the spring,
Amidst the gratitude of grass,
Bluebells that rapturously ring.
A weeping tree will stop his axe,
So he will heat his hut with dung,
Not hunt, for all the hunted's sakes,
Say, no, these hens' necks won't be wrung.
Though if he has a family
To forage food and fuel for,
He will be forced to chop down trees,
To choke and shoot, to flay and gut,
To flesh a spit unfeelingly,
To fill a fire pit in the floor.
It dulls his spirit, it destroys
It, his shamanic ear will shut,
What would have been an augury
Will only be his own advice
And when most asked for, most awry.
His village will be stones and ice.

Those mountain men, the Khevsurs, wore
    Crusaders' surcoats, white and red,
And chain mail… What, for fuck's sake, for?
No one wore chain mail any more,
    But they did, even on the head.

They also wore a banderole
    Of brassy cartridges, a belt
With pistols in the belly's roll,
A musket on a sling, a whole
    Canteen of cutlery, a pelt.

They were too tough to get called out
    As fashionistas or as fops.
Chain mail, though, what was that about?
Bullets shoot through it like *sauerkraut*…
    That was their style. Style never stops.

ès

The few days that I stayed there for, so beautiful a base,
    In one of those stone towers in Shatili, showed me how

The power that some places have is in that pride of place
    That those have who have hewn the stone and whose
                             heirs own it now.

ès

The house had seven wooden chests,
    With carvings of the zodiac
To ward off those unwelcome guests,
    The ghosts of lucklessness and lack.

The chest that had the daily flour
    Was in a corner, fingered white,
The chest with all their clothes, full for
    A family, was roped down tight.

A small chest, in a smoky nook,
    Was for what they did not yet know,
A big chest, by the door, for crook-
    Ed curios, like clogs for snow.

The chest that had the Sunday flour
    Had been anointed by the priests,
As had the old chest, sunk in the floor,
    That had the sacred bread for feasts.

The lady of the house would kneel
    In front of either holy chest,
Under an icon on a nail,
    And eat a seed that had been blessed.

A cowbell concert through the guesthouse win-
    Dow and the dusk is darkening a won-
        Derful Old Master's wattle, rut and wain.

                  ❧

Shall we talk too about the turs,
    Straggling on the western slopes,
    That are half goats, half antelopes?

They hide from hunters, from the towers,
    Grazing at midnight, on low leaves and grass,
    Dozing at midday, down a crevasse.

They are endangered now, the turs,
    Lynxes and wolves, that they are prey
    Of, too, in this less wild array.

They hide from hikers, from the tours,
    Turning their horns for their admir-
    Ing only, like a living lyre.

                  ❧

IV

∪

Some sort of summer colony, I thought,
With iron awnings, elegantly wrought,
Tables and chairs. They dine *al fresco* here.
The tables, made of matt-black marble, had
A bygone grandeur, from before the year
An era ended and the world went mad.
Edwardian in England, a resort
That had a windy promenade and pier.
Or more Victorian. A certain gloom.

It was a cemetery. With a tomb
At every table. See that seating plan!
Chairs, tables, tombs. The tomb is at the head.

They dine here with the dead. They feed the dead.
This era is a lot more bygone than
The 1900s, it is Neolithic.
Does it appease them? Doing what their an-
Cestors once did. Communing with the mythic,
With the momentous, with the monolithic.

❧

Something was wrong. The driver drew the reins.
　　The two white horses of the carriage stopped,
Facing the forest, where the road still runs.
　　Somebody pointed. Men, like poachers, stepped

Out from the trees with rifles and took aim.
　　His wife, who sat beside him, counted. Six
Assassins. She remembered that. They came
　　Closer, shouting for calm, for all their sakes,

And shot the poet. Six shots in the chest.
　　Wings disentangled, flapping through the leaves
In frills of shock. His wife sobbed. No one chased
　　The gang of gunmen. There were other lives.

❧

Wilder than Wilde was, Titsian, a pasha of a po-
Et, in a kaftan, was a poet out of Poe,

As Persian in his poems as Parisian,
In whose eyes, aching up, Mount Kazbek was Parnassian.

A cup of coffee had a prophecy of something brown.
The grounds of it inspired a paradisal brain.

❧

Nothing, if not for love, is, not
    A poppy nodding on a path,
A line of this, a lovely note,
        A panther padding, no ringed plov-
    Ers paddling, no pips, no pith,
       No, nothing is, if not for love.

And of all loves, autumnal love's
    Tonality is thinning out,
A tart wind tearing off the leaves,
      Until, oh, there is no disguise
    On any twig, no layer of doubt,
       And love is not and nothing is.

ɞ

And on the holy mountain they are howling at the moon,
   On a big dipper, on a ferris wheel.

   The poets lying there are listening. The wail.
They wonder what it is, what it might mean.

The Mtkvari is a mile of moonlight. So much moan-
   Ing, in the valley, in the alleys. While

   All things on earth this night will not be well,
What will be, still, is Mtatsminda and the moon.

ɞ

He said that poets don't write poems, they
    Are written by them, rushed on, like a land-
Slide, roughing out a draft at night, the thy-
    Roid throbbing, as a book of frowns is lined.

In the old orchards apple-white was falling
    And on his lips and tongue the reddish stains
        Of Georgian soil were kisses by the sun.

Literary executors were filing.
    A landslide, oh, a mountain raining stones,
        A landslide would unwrite the poets soon.

༄

Georgians beware of Georgians. They were their
    Own enemies. Orjonikidze, Ber-
        Ia and the biggest, with his *nom de guerre*.

༄

Ը

His pen's nib was a songbird's beak,
   Scratching a stanza on a bleached-
White sheet, as bleak as that blank peak,

    With ink that was a Black Sea blue,
  As blue as when the Argo beached.
    The bird sings inconsolably.

He wrote about a burning bull,
   Its calling, its communion.
The bull is incorruptible.

    Beaters were beating poetry
  Up in the Writers' Union.
    He was his hunting gun's true prey.

※

The night and I can now confide. That mountain has a
                                                           mine
It brings its bags of moonlight from. This is a map of mine.

It hears it throbbing through my ribs. As fiercely as a fist
Against a door at four a.m.. Who heard it for the first

Time has a seam of moonlight in here, that the night and I
Won't tell you any more about. I say a name and die.

※

Galaktioni, what a poet, was
    The greatest of a wasted generation,
With odes, oneiric odes, awash with wooz-
    Y iteration and alliteration,
Like horses' manes in morning mist, a wiz-
    Ened tree hand warning of obliteration.

Beria beat him badly, very badly…
    Galaktioni, tongue-tied, stiff and gaunt,
Wasn't the same, more solitary, sadly
    An alcoholic, whose nocturnal haunt
Was an asylum, maybe not so madly
    Amidst that madness, untruth and its taunt.

Olga, his wife, of good Old Bolsheviks,
    Was trucked off to an icy camp and died.
His cousin Titsian (For what? A vex-
    Ing verse?) was tortured to admit a deed
No Dadaist would do. And shot. Like vacc-
    Inating… Writers, friends, so many dead.

Galaktioni was the one they trust-
    Ed, as their witness, with his shattered stare,
The silence of it, swelling with disgust,
    With their bile too, big throatfuls, with despair,
Until he jumped, as any poet must,
    Through a blue window into empty air.

ஐ

Shutting out Russian power, circuits shorting,
 For a free Georgia, was exciting. Shouting
  And shooting in the air, then shooting, shooting…

     ಎ

A prophet for a president?
 And a professor and a poet, oh,
And paranoid. I don't
 Think this will end well. Two
  Years later. No, it didn't. They were woeful years.

A playwright? Who robbed banks (like Joe).
 And on the ruling council? I
Have written plays (what joy)
 And have a question. Why?
  This didn't end well either. They were woeful
          years.

     ಎ

They shouted it across the street,
 The electricity was on,
  For a few hours, three or four,
 On some days and on others none,

And then they dashed in, doing straight-
 Away the things they needed most,
  Washing machines or showers or
 Phoning… This isn't what is missed.

Food without fridges, sating strong-
    Er stomachs' summer appetites,
        And iced as only winter ices,
   Unheated rooms and unlit nights.

This was an era, not so long
    Ago, that wasn't electronic,
        Wasn't devoted to devices,
   The egocentric and ironic.

                                    ಶ.

The roses were romantic. The reforms
    Were realistic, though. A new police
        Force. Fewer regulations. There were horns

Of plenty honking, peeping, now the norms
    Were Western. And investment did increase.
        So what went wrong? The roses. There were
                                            thorns.

                                    ಶ.

And then there was a war, a little war,
    That most of us in Europe weren't aware
        Of. Air strikes. Occupation. There they were.

                                    ಶ.

A *grande salle* (ah, but flakey paint), a long brass chandelier,
    An icon shot with agates of an aura-armoured saint,
And, yes, amidst this art there is another era here,
    Attendants as in Auden and a four year old's complaint.

                    ಌ

I see an open-ended house,
    With bricks, then plaster, then a smear
        Like a bird's, a plastic sheet, a hole.
    A husband and wife are living here
With children in the shadows, whose
        House is a castle on a hill.

I see a sad old glass façade,
    A jagged jigsaw, pieces missing
        Someone has looked for everywhere.
A line of clothes is hung inside,
        As if a roofed-in run of air
      Is right for drying, rain clouds massing.

I see a breeze-block balcony,
    Above a path of mud and dung,
      A balustrade of pallet wood,
    With metal poles like scaffolding,
A sofa ripped across the knee…
      A balcony and life is good.

                    ಌ

And in the maddest minibus,
    Round mountain bends, two men start singing,
With so much mettle, so much bass,
    The bus itself is ringing, ringing.

And in the little cuckoo train's
    Carriage the ringtones have stopped ringing,
Because of this, the softer strains
    Of three young women singing, singing.

                          ଈ

I stride out/slow down on the famous four
    Day hike towards Ushguli, wet and urgh
For two days, with a stream too fast for for-
    Ding, then, ah, sunny, a huge glacier,
Butterflies, rhododendrons, summits far
    More beautiful than I had read they were.
        The ending of it is a fairytale
        That those who live there feel, for all its toll.

Ushguli was a summer residence
    For Queen Tamar. A tower and some walls
Are hers, in ruins on a hilltop, dense
    With weeds, where courtiers once used their wiles,
Yes, Rustaveli too, whose lines condense
    These folded valleys and the wind that wails.
        A yellow fresco of Tamar above
        An entrance is an image of his love.

I see the ranges that inspired him, hear
    The roaring of the rivers that inspired
Him. And what he inspires. His code is clear.
    To be a friend. No hardship to be spared.
To be hospitable. And not to fear
    It failing. There is more if more is poured.
        This is the mindset now. The generos-
        Ity of Georgians nothing can erase.

I think how kind it was of Ana to
    Hand me a grand edition of *The Knight*
And how the house of Abashidze, *tou-*
    T en gentillesse, had room for one more night
(Yes, these are the acknowledgements and too
    Many to mention, kindnesses unit-
        Ing young and old, a small farm's host, her own
        Cow's milk, an Instagramming Anglophone).

And what I hope, for all of them, is this,
    That Georgia will develop well, that it
Will be sustainable and fair, with sys-
    Tematic local input and, polit-
Ically, parties with ideas, Swiss-
    Like in its borders, that won't move a bit,
        And that it will, whatever, always feel
        Welcoming, wonky, oh, and wonderful.

                                ès

Notes

I

This bubble round a rock is blown by Barbale

Barbale (*bar-bah-leh*) is a goddess of the sun.

The king of Colchis asked

The classical kingdom of Colchis was on the territory that is now Georgia.

She came from Cappadocia

Saint Nino converted the king of Iberia (East Georgia) in 327, after which Christianity became the national religion.

The A script of the alphabet

The Georgian alphabet has three scripts, *asomtavruli* (which means *capital letters* and is the script used here), *nuskhuri*, which was also a clerical script, and *mkhedruli* (which means *cavalry*), a civil script which became standard.

Great iron gates across a mountain pass

There were fortifications on the passes of Derbent and Darial in the Caucasus to protect against invasion from the north. The legendary iron gates supposedly dated back to the time of Alexander the Great.

And in Gelati's gateway I

King Davit Aghmashenebeli (David the Builder) was Georgia's greatest king. He was buried in the gateway of Gelati monastery, where he had founded an academy.

A city hidden in a mountainside

The cave city of Vardzia was hidden underground until an earthquake in 1283 sheered off the hillside. The valley of the Kura river below it was a highway for invading armies.

I wander through the ruins of the palace

Queen Tamar was Georgia's greatest ruler (sorry, David). She ruled from 1178 to 1213, at the height of Georgia's Golden Age.

Shota Rustaveli wrote Georgia's great epic poem *The Knight In The Panther Skin* during or shortly after her reign.

II

The poems in this part draw on *The Knight In The Panther Skin* (see the previous note).

A poem that is long, like this

See stanzas 12-14. This poem is written in an iambic equivalent of the *shairi* form used by Rustaveli. Georgian is an unstressed language, like French, so its metre is syllabic. *Shairi* lines have 16 syllables (8 beats in the iambic equivalent) with a *caesura* in the middle. There are four lines per stanza, all with the same rhyme.

This is what love ideally is

See stanzas 20-24.

The tiny, tiny, Tinatin

See stanzas 34-37 and 41-42. Tamar co-ruled with her father for six years before ruling on her own after his death. Tinatin means *sunbeam*.

A lion and a lioness

See stanza 40.

A knight sat sobbing by a stream

See stanzas 86-100 and 131-137. *What ailed the pale knight loitering* is from Keats' poem *La Belle Dame Sans Merci*.

For Avtandil to fail to find

See stanzas 187 and 201-234.

The sobbing knight was Tariel

See stanzas 263-289 and 307-314.

Her name was Nestan-Darejan

See stanzas 347-351, 383-385, 426-429, 445-457 and 470-473.

The old king told the court his news

See stanzas 513-518, 528-529, 548-549 and 563-587. Her aunt is the widow of a Kaji, a race of sorcerers with demonic powers.

The third tall knight, a prince, was Pri-

See stanzas 599-604, 617-618 and 628-634. Pridon is pronounced *preedon*.

Then Avtandil rode sadly home

See stanzas 677, 700-708 and 822. *Aloe tree* is an epithet Rustaveli uses to describe his heroes (and heroines).

He knew the madness of the moon

See stanza 848.

With Nestan's knight too stressed now from

See stanzas 942, 977-979, 1031 and 1069-1073.

The woman was a merchant's wife

See stanzas 1079, 1084-1088, 1092-1094, 1099-1102 and 1272-1276. I have changed the order in which they tell their stories. In Rustaveli's poem, Patman tells her story after Avtandil has murdered someone for her. Then Avtandil tells his story, then Patman helps him.

That night, her feelings were forlorn

See stanzas 1136-1143, 1152–1154, 1177, 1199-1209, 1233-1241 and 1248-1251. The *casement* stanza is from Keats' poem *Ode To A Nightingale*.

And in the forest grotto's fort

See stanzas 1372-1379.

The three knights, with three hundred men

See stanzas 1396-1398 and 1419-1429.

They celebrated their success

See stanzas 1444-1447, 1455-1457, 1557-1567, 1644-1645 and 1655-1656.

III

The Georgian Lady, she was called

Gürcü Hatun (*Georgian Lady* in Turkish) was a 13th Century Georgian princess who was married to the Sultan of Rum, Kaykhusraw II.

The log fire in his study blazes

After the failure of the 1832 plot against Russian rule, Alexander Chavchavadze burnt all the poems he had written from 1820 to 1832, destroying any evidence that might incriminate him.

General. Poet. And why not?

Grigol Orbeliani was a Romantic poet, a Georgian patriot and a high-ranking officer in the Tsarist army and administration. He wrote *A Toast, or A Night Feast After A Battle Near Yerevan*.

What might the Mtkvari river write

See *Thoughts On The Banks Of The Mtkvari* by Nikoloz Baratashvili.

A shepherdess was storm-struck on

See *The Hermit* by Ilia Chavchavadze.

Ah, attar in the air, a crims-

See *Suliko* by Akaki Tsereteli.

I wish I was the rain, the rain

See *Why Was I Created Human?* by Vazha-Pshavela.

In that hard highland, where the win-

See *Aluda Ketelauri* by Vazha-Pshavela.

A sprig of violets sprang up

See *Despair* by Vazha-Pshavela.

A man who eats the meat of snakes

See *The Snake Eater* by Vazha-Pshavela.

IV

Something was wrong. The driver drew the reins

Ilia Chavchavadze was assassinated in 1907.

Wilder than Wilde was, Titsian, a pasha of a po-

See *Self-Portrait* by Titsian Tabidze.

Nothing, if not for love, is, not

See *Without Love* by Galaktion Tabidze.

And on the holy mountain they are howling at the moon

See *The Moon Over Mtatsminda* by Galaktion Tabidze. Overlooking Tbilisi, Mtatsminda means *holy mountain*. A funicular was built up it in 1905 and an amusement park on top in the 1930s. The Mtatsminda Pantheon of poets (including Galaktion Tabidze and Nikoloz Baratashvili) and others is halfway up the ascent.

He said that poets don't write poems, they

See *Poem Landslide* by Titsian Tabidze.

His pen's nib was a songbird's beak

Paolo Iashvili shot himself with a hunting rifle during a session in the Writers' Union building in Tbilisi in 1937. See *Desk — My Parnassus* and *Red Bull*.

The night and I can now confide. That mountain has a mine

See *The Night And I* by Galaktion Tabidze.

Galaktioni, what a poet, was

See *Blue Horses* by Galaktion Tabidze, who is known simply

as Galaktioni. He committed suicide in 1959. Olga Okujava, his wife, was arrested in 1937 and died in 1944. Titsian Tabidze was executed in 1937.

And then there was a war, a little war

In the August 2008 war, the Russian army occupied the cities of Zugdidi, Gori and Poti.

A *grande salle* (ah, but flakey paint), a long brass chandelier

Loosely based on Kutaisi State Historical Museum. It is in a neoclassical building that used to be the Bank of Georgia. The bystanders are from Auden's poem *Musée Des Beaux Arts*.

I stride out/slow down on the famous four

The fresco of Queen Tamar is in the Lamaria church in Ushguli.

Reading

The Knight In The Panther Skin by Shota Rustaveli, translated by Lyn Coffin

Georgian Poetry, Rustaveli to Galaktion, translated by Lyn Coffin

Georgian Poetry, translated by Donald Rayfield, Diana Russell, Venera Urushadze, Walter May

The Literature Of Georgia by Donald Rayfield

There are also some translations of Georgian poetry available online, in particular Rebecca Gould's translations of poems by Titsian Tabidze and Paolo Iashvili.

A Georgian Anthology

Andrew Staniland's *A Georgian Anthology* is a sequence of poems inspired by the classical myths about Prometheus and Colchis, by Georgia's own mythology and history, by its poetry, especially Shota Rustaveli's *The Knight In The Panther Skin*, and by the beauty of the Georgian landscape, with its castles, towers, monasteries and the mountains of the Caucasus.

Letters Of Introduction (2018)

Andrew Staniland's *Letters Of Introduction (2018)* includes a series of odes, four *Sonnets On Public Life* and a series of *Three-Line Variations* that are an English lyrical equivalent of *haiku*. There are poems about post-truth politics and #MeToo, as well as poems about Armenia, written before the April 2018 revolution, including a sequence, *Thirty-Nine Letters*, that has a poem for each letter of the Armenian alphabet.

Playful Poems (2016)

Andrew Staniland's *Playful Poems (2016)* is a sequence of over a hundred short poems written between March 2015 and August 2016 and prompted by reading most of Shakespeare's plays in their likely chronological order. There are poems about the wars in Ukraine and Syria, refugees, dictators, nationalism and Brexit, as well as *The lovely wood of piebald light/That any English poem is*.

Rhapsodies (2014)

Andrew Staniland's *Rhapsodies (2014)* takes its title from the verse form of the two long poems at its centre, *Rhapsody* and *Corona Lumina*, written in long rhyming couplets. The same verse form is used for a poem about the Ukrainian musicians *Dakh Daughters* and Valentin Silvestrov. There are translations from Russian and Ukrainian, a tribute to Seamus Heaney and a sequence of short poems about an album by the French singer-songwriter Amélie-les-crayons.

The Perennial Poetry (2010)

Andrew Staniland's *The Perennial Poetry (2010)* is a collection of contemporary English Romantic poetry written in classical metre. There are poems about spiritual experience, creativity, love and poetry itself. The subjects include contemporary films and paintings, Chartres cathedral and the war in Afghanistan, a trip to Tallinn and writing a themed poem for a poetry competition. There are odes and sonnets, including translations of French, Spanish, Italian and German sonnets.

Two Story Poems (2009)

Andrew Staniland's *Two Story Poems (2009)* are original stories in classical verse. *A Human Disguise* is a spiritual comedy set in ancient India. A minor god takes on human form to hide from a demon who is chasing him. *Compassion* is a ghost story set in medieval Japan. A *samurai* gains a supernatural power that is too terrible for him to use.

Hymns, Films And Sonnetinas (2007)

Andrew Staniland's *Hymns, Films And Sonnetinas (2007)* are written in classical metre, in the romantic tradition of English poetry. They include *Five Hymns* (dedicated to five gods and goddesses representing different elements of contemporary culture and spirituality), *Twelve Films By Eric Rohmer*, *An Older Actress* (a narrative poem in alexandrine couplets about a French actress and her film career), *William Blake And The Eighteenth Century New Age* and *Sonnetinas* (a miscellaneous sequence of sonnet-like miniatures).

NEW POEMS (2006)

The poems in Andrew Staniland's *New Poems (2006)* are poems about contemporary spiritual experience, written in classical metre, in the romantic tradition of English poetry. They include a series of odes and a sequence of short poems which give the collection its title.

The Beauty Of Psyche (2005)

Andrew Staniland's prose-poem novel *The Beauty Of Psyche (2005)* is a retelling of the Greek myth of Cupid and Psyche as a novel about imagination. The characters are played by actors, against a backdrop of paintings, models and sets. The story at times becomes a series of paintings and sculptures in an exhibition. And the references to people, films, theatre and other myths may or may not be imaginary too.

THE WEIGHT OF LIGHT (2004)

Andrew Staniland's prose-poem novel *The Weight Of Light (2004)* is a lyrical description of the inner life and spiritual practice of Delphine, a Frenchwoman living in London. It is set entirely in her apartment, like a camera recording the poetry of her daily life, her meditations and spiritual experiences. It is a "new spirituality" novel that is both literary and an honest description of a contemporary spiritual life.

Three Cine-Poems (1997)

The three cine-poems collected here use classical blank verse and contemporary cinematic narrative techniques to tell their stories.

White Russian (1995) is a lyrical description of a young Russian woman's life in London.

A Child Of God (1996) is a comic study of a New Age guru and his small band of devotees.

A European Master (1997) is a debate about contemporary aesthetic values between a French actress and an East European film director.

POEMS (1982-2004)

This is a collection of Andrew Staniland's poems from 1982 to 2004. Some are written in free verse, some in metric verse. They are in the romantic tradition of English poetry and explore contemporary spiritual and psychotherapeutic experience.

Four Plays (1994)

The Temple Of The Goddess (1992) is a verse tragedy set in pre-classical Greece. A matriarchal bronze age state is invaded by a patriarchal iron age army.

The Playwright (1993) is a drama about resurgent nationalism in post-communist Eastern Europe.

Mornings In The Life Of A Theatre Critic (1993) is a London theatre comedy.

The Valley Of Stones (1994) is a tragedy of survival and defiance in a refugee camp.

Printed in Great Britain
by Amazon